# Home Maintenance Log For

Address:

_____

_____

Date of Purchase:

_____

# DEDICATION

This Home Maintenance Checklist book is dedicated to all the energetic and hard working people out there who want to take care of their home and document the process.

You are my inspiration for producing books and I'm honored to be a part of keeping all of your Home Maintenance notes and records organized.

This journal notebook will help you record your details about the tasks you perform with your home upkeep.

Thoughtfully put together with these sections to record: Monthly Systems Maintenance, Repairman Contact, Home Warranty Information, Appliance Information, Appliance Repair Log, Monthly Maintenance Log, Quarterly Maintenance Log, Yearly Maintenance Log & Notes.

# HOW TO USE THIS BOOK

The purpose of this book is to keep all of your Home Maintenance notes all in one place. It will help keep you organized.

This Home Maintenance Journal will allow you to accurately document every detail about your maintenance and your tasks. It's a great way to chart your course through keeping a beautiful home.

Here are examples of the prompts for you to fill in and write about your experience in this book:

1. Monthly Systems Maintenance - Each month of the year has a different checklist so you never forget anything. Some examples are: clean pipes, check roof for soft spots, check gutters, inspect attic, change air filters, check pantry for expired food, furnace tune-up, winterize AC, vacuum frig coils, and much, much more.

2. Repairman Contact - Company or Individual Name, Phone Number, Email, Technician Name

3. Home Warranty Information - Company Name, Premium Paid, Contract Length, Policy Number, User Name, Password. Each system & Appliance has a section to check if it's covered. Also a usage log for date, what was serviced & what the problem was.

4. Appliance Information - Date of Purchase, Purchased From, Price, Serial Number, Warranty.

5. Appliance Repair Log - Date of Service, Appliance, Repairman, Contact Info, Cost, Warranty.

6. Monthly Maintenance Log - For example, checking smoke detectors & changing furnace filter, etc.

7. Quarterly Maintenance Log - For example, check basement/ crawl space for leaks, check shower/sink drains, seasonal tasks, etc.

8. Yearly Maintenance Log - For example, smoke detector batteries, carbon monoxide detector, etc.

9. Notes - Plenty of blank lined pages of notes for any other important information or details such as your projects for the household like building a wheelchair ramp or playset, checklist for any specific room in your home that you may want to add, list of weekly chores for each member of the family or an improvement wish list.

# Systems Maintenance By Month

## JANUARY

- Clean Pipes (Descale overnight)
- Clean Showerheads and Taps
- Clean and Recaulk Shower/Sinks
- Clear Ice Dams In Gutters

## FEBRUARY

- Deep Clean Oven and Stovetop
- Clean Washer
- Clean Dyer and Check Vent
- Clean Dishwasher & Check Filter

## MARCH

- Deep Spring Clean
- Check Roof for Soft Spots
- Check Sump Pump
- Clean Gutters

# Systems Maintenance By Month

| APRIL |
|---|
| Spring Clean Kitchen |
| Vacuum HVAC Unit |
| Inspect Attic |
| Have AC Tuned |
|  |

| MAY |
|---|
| Check Exhaust Fans |
| Check Ceiling Fan Blades/Dust |
| Check Weather Stripping |
| Fix Rust Spots |
|  |

| JUNE |
|---|
| Clean Window Wells |
| Remove Dead Limbs From Trees |
| Touchup Paint |
| Remove Dead Plants From Flowerbeds |
|  |

# Systems Maintenance By Month

## JULY

- Clean/Stain Deck
- Maintain Garage Door
- Power Wash Concrete
- Check Ductwork for Leaks

## AUGUST

- Clean Garbage Disposal
- Clean Out Freezer
- Clean Window Treatments
- Change Air Filters

## SEPTEMBER

- Flush Water Heater
- Furnace Tune-Up
- Check Pantry for Expired Food
- Check Carbon Monoxide Detectors

# Systems Maintenance By Month

| OCTOBER |
| --- |
| Remove Exterior Hoses & Drain |
| Vacuum & Clean Furnace |
| Deep Clean Microwave |
| Winterize AC |
|  |

| NOVEMBER |
| --- |
| Vacuum Fridge Coils |
| Deep Clean Fridge |
| Clean Fridge Drain Pan |
| Clean Circuit Breakers |
|  |

| DECEMBER |
| --- |
| Test Electrical Outlets |
| Run Water in Unused Rooms |
| Inspect Fire Extinguishers |
| Replace Smoke Detector Batteries |
|  |

# Repairman Contact Information

Company Name: _____
Phone Number: _____
Email: _____
Technician Name: _____


Company Name: _____
Phone Number: _____
Email: _____
Technician Name: _____


Company Name: _____
Phone Number: _____
Email: _____
Technician Name: _____


Company Name: _____
Phone Number: _____
Email: _____
Technician Name: _____

# Repairman Contact Information

Company Name:_____
Phone Number:_____
Email:_____
Technician Name:_____


Company Name:_____
Phone Number:_____
Email:_____
Technician Name:_____


Company Name:_____
Phone Number:_____
Email:_____
Technician Name:_____


Company Name:_____
Phone Number:_____
Email:_____
Technician Name:_____

# Repairman Contact Information

Company Name:_____
Phone Number:_____
Email:_____
Technician Name:_____


Company Name:_____
Phone Number:_____
Email:_____
Technician Name:_____


Company Name:_____
Phone Number:_____
Email:_____
Technician Name:_____


Company Name:_____
Phone Number:_____
Email:_____
Technician Name:_____

# Home Warranty Information:

Company:_____

Premium Paid:_____

Contract Length:_____

Policy Number:_____

Customer Service Number:_____

Online Login User Name:_____

Online Login Password:_____

## Appliances Covered:

|  |  |  |  |
|---|---|---|---|
|  | Refrigerator |  | Ice Maker |
|  | Stove |  | Garbage Disposal |
|  | Washer |  | Other |
|  | Dryer |  | Other |
|  | Dishwasher |  | Other |
|  | Built-In Microwave |  | Other |
|  | Trash Compactor |  | Other |

# Home Warranty Information (Continued):

## Systems Covered:

| | | | |
|---|---|---|---|
| | Air Conditioning | | Central Vac. |
| | Heating | | Septic Pump |
| | Electrical | | Well Pump |
| | Door Bell | | Other |
| | Smoke Detectors | | Other |
| | Ceiling Fans | | Other |
| | Water Heater | | Other |

## Usage Log:

| Date | What Was Serviced | Problem | Service Technician |
|---|---|---|---|
| | | | |
| | | | |
| | | | |
| | | | |
| | | | |
| | | | |
| | | | |

# Home Warranty Information (Continued):

| Date | What Was Serviced | Problem | Service Technician |
|------|-------------------|---------|--------------------|
|      |                   |         |                    |
|      |                   |         |                    |
|      |                   |         |                    |
|      |                   |         |                    |
|      |                   |         |                    |
|      |                   |         |                    |
|      |                   |         |                    |
|      |                   |         |                    |
|      |                   |         |                    |
|      |                   |         |                    |
|      |                   |         |                    |
|      |                   |         |                    |
|      |                   |         |                    |
|      |                   |         |                    |
|      |                   |         |                    |
|      |                   |         |                    |

# Appliance Information

| Date of Purchase | Appliance | Purchased From | Price | Serial Number | Warranty |
|---|---|---|---|---|---|
| | | | | | |
| | | | | | |
| | | | | | |
| | | | | | |
| | | | | | |
| | | | | | |
| | | | | | |
| | | | | | |
| | | | | | |
| | | | | | |
| | | | | | |
| | | | | | |
| | | | | | |
| | | | | | |
| | | | | | |
| | | | | | |
| | | | | | |

# Appliance Information

| Date of Purchase | Appliance | Purchased From | Price | Serial Number | Warranty |
|---|---|---|---|---|---|
| | | | | | |
| | | | | | |
| | | | | | |
| | | | | | |
| | | | | | |
| | | | | | |
| | | | | | |
| | | | | | |
| | | | | | |
| | | | | | |
| | | | | | |
| | | | | | |
| | | | | | |
| | | | | | |
| | | | | | |
| | | | | | |
| | | | | | |

# Appliance Information

| Date of Purchase | Appliance | Purchased From | Price | Serial Number | Warranty |
|---|---|---|---|---|---|
| | | | | | |
| | | | | | |
| | | | | | |
| | | | | | |
| | | | | | |
| | | | | | |
| | | | | | |
| | | | | | |
| | | | | | |
| | | | | | |
| | | | | | |
| | | | | | |
| | | | | | |
| | | | | | |
| | | | | | |
| | | | | | |
| | | | | | |

# Appliance Repair Log

| Date of Service | Appliance | Repairman | Contact Info | Cost | Warranty |
|---|---|---|---|---|---|
| | | | | | |
| | | | | | |
| | | | | | |
| | | | | | |
| | | | | | |
| | | | | | |
| | | | | | |
| | | | | | |
| | | | | | |
| | | | | | |
| | | | | | |
| | | | | | |
| | | | | | |
| | | | | | |
| | | | | | |
| | | | | | |
| | | | | | |

# Appliance Repair Log

| Date of Service | Appliance | Repairman | Contact Info | Cost | Warranty |
|---|---|---|---|---|---|
| | | | | | |
| | | | | | |
| | | | | | |
| | | | | | |
| | | | | | |
| | | | | | |
| | | | | | |
| | | | | | |
| | | | | | |
| | | | | | |
| | | | | | |
| | | | | | |
| | | | | | |
| | | | | | |
| | | | | | |
| | | | | | |
| | | | | | |

# Appliance Repair Log

| Date of Service | Appliance | Repairman | Contact Info | Cost | Warranty |
|---|---|---|---|---|---|
| | | | | | |
| | | | | | |
| | | | | | |
| | | | | | |
| | | | | | |
| | | | | | |
| | | | | | |
| | | | | | |
| | | | | | |
| | | | | | |
| | | | | | |
| | | | | | |
| | | | | | |
| | | | | | |
| | | | | | |
| | | | | | |
| | | | | | |

# Monthly Maintenance Log

| Date | Check Smoke Detectors | Change Furnace Filter | Other: | Other: | Performed By (Initials) |
|------|----------------------|----------------------|--------|--------|------------------------|
|      |                      |                      |        |        |                        |
|      |                      |                      |        |        |                        |
|      |                      |                      |        |        |                        |
|      |                      |                      |        |        |                        |
|      |                      |                      |        |        |                        |
|      |                      |                      |        |        |                        |
|      |                      |                      |        |        |                        |
|      |                      |                      |        |        |                        |
|      |                      |                      |        |        |                        |
|      |                      |                      |        |        |                        |
|      |                      |                      |        |        |                        |
|      |                      |                      |        |        |                        |
|      |                      |                      |        |        |                        |
|      |                      |                      |        |        |                        |
|      |                      |                      |        |        |                        |
|      |                      |                      |        |        |                        |
|      |                      |                      |        |        |                        |

# Monthly Maintenance Log

| Date | Check Smoke Detectors | Change Furnace Filter | Other: | Other: | Performed By (Initials) |
|------|----------------------|----------------------|--------|--------|------------------------|
|      |                      |                      |        |        |                        |
|      |                      |                      |        |        |                        |
|      |                      |                      |        |        |                        |
|      |                      |                      |        |        |                        |
|      |                      |                      |        |        |                        |
|      |                      |                      |        |        |                        |
|      |                      |                      |        |        |                        |
|      |                      |                      |        |        |                        |
|      |                      |                      |        |        |                        |
|      |                      |                      |        |        |                        |
|      |                      |                      |        |        |                        |
|      |                      |                      |        |        |                        |
|      |                      |                      |        |        |                        |
|      |                      |                      |        |        |                        |
|      |                      |                      |        |        |                        |
|      |                      |                      |        |        |                        |
|      |                      |                      |        |        |                        |

# Monthly Maintenance Log

| Date | Check Smoke Detectors | Change Furnace Filter | Other: | Other: | Performed By (Initials) |
|------|------|------|------|------|------|
|      |      |      |      |      |      |
|      |      |      |      |      |      |
|      |      |      |      |      |      |
|      |      |      |      |      |      |
|      |      |      |      |      |      |
|      |      |      |      |      |      |
|      |      |      |      |      |      |
|      |      |      |      |      |      |
|      |      |      |      |      |      |
|      |      |      |      |      |      |
|      |      |      |      |      |      |
|      |      |      |      |      |      |
|      |      |      |      |      |      |
|      |      |      |      |      |      |
|      |      |      |      |      |      |
|      |      |      |      |      |      |
|      |      |      |      |      |      |

# Quarterly Maintenance Log

| Date | Check Basement/Crawl Space For Leaks | Clean Fridge | Clean Baseboards | Check Shower/Sink Drain Issues | Performed By (Initials) |
|------|--------------------------------------|--------------|------------------|--------------------------------|-------------------------|
|      |                                      |              |                  |                                |                         |
|      |                                      |              |                  |                                |                         |
|      |                                      |              |                  |                                |                         |
|      |                                      |              |                  |                                |                         |
|      |                                      |              |                  |                                |                         |
|      |                                      |              |                  |                                |                         |
|      |                                      |              |                  |                                |                         |
|      |                                      |              |                  |                                |                         |
|      |                                      |              |                  |                                |                         |
|      |                                      |              |                  |                                |                         |
|      |                                      |              |                  |                                |                         |
|      |                                      |              |                  |                                |                         |
|      |                                      |              |                  |                                |                         |
|      |                                      |              |                  |                                |                         |
|      |                                      |              |                  |                                |                         |
|      |                                      |              |                  |                                |                         |
|      |                                      |              |                  |                                |                         |

# Quarterly Maintenance Log

| Date | Check Basement/Crawl Space For Leaks | Clean Fridge | Clean Baseboards | Check Shower/Sink Drain Issues | Performed By (Initials) |
|------|--------------------------------------|--------------|------------------|-------------------------------|-------------------------|
|      |                                      |              |                  |                               |                         |
|      |                                      |              |                  |                               |                         |
|      |                                      |              |                  |                               |                         |
|      |                                      |              |                  |                               |                         |
|      |                                      |              |                  |                               |                         |
|      |                                      |              |                  |                               |                         |
|      |                                      |              |                  |                               |                         |
|      |                                      |              |                  |                               |                         |
|      |                                      |              |                  |                               |                         |
|      |                                      |              |                  |                               |                         |
|      |                                      |              |                  |                               |                         |
|      |                                      |              |                  |                               |                         |
|      |                                      |              |                  |                               |                         |
|      |                                      |              |                  |                               |                         |
|      |                                      |              |                  |                               |                         |
|      |                                      |              |                  |                               |                         |
|      |                                      |              |                  |                               |                         |

# Quarterly Maintenance Log

| Date | Check Basement/Crawl Space For Leaks | Clean Fridge | Clean Baseboards | Check Shower/Sink Drain Issues | Performed By (Initials) |
|---|---|---|---|---|---|
| | | | | | |
| | | | | | |
| | | | | | |
| | | | | | |
| | | | | | |
| | | | | | |
| | | | | | |
| | | | | | |
| | | | | | |
| | | | | | |
| | | | | | |
| | | | | | |
| | | | | | |
| | | | | | |
| | | | | | |
| | | | | | |
| | | | | | |

# Yearly Maintenance Log

| Date | Smoke Detector Batteries | Carbon Monoxide Detector | Clean Gutters | Other: | Other: | Performed By (Initials) |
|------|--------------------------|--------------------------|---------------|--------|--------|-------------------------|
|      |                          |                          |               |        |        |                         |
|      |                          |                          |               |        |        |                         |
|      |                          |                          |               |        |        |                         |
|      |                          |                          |               |        |        |                         |
|      |                          |                          |               |        |        |                         |
|      |                          |                          |               |        |        |                         |
|      |                          |                          |               |        |        |                         |
|      |                          |                          |               |        |        |                         |
|      |                          |                          |               |        |        |                         |
|      |                          |                          |               |        |        |                         |
|      |                          |                          |               |        |        |                         |
|      |                          |                          |               |        |        |                         |
|      |                          |                          |               |        |        |                         |
|      |                          |                          |               |        |        |                         |
|      |                          |                          |               |        |        |                         |
|      |                          |                          |               |        |        |                         |
|      |                          |                          |               |        |        |                         |

# Yearly Maintenance Log

| Date | Smoke Detector Batteries | Carbon Monoxide Detector | Clean Gutters | Other: | Other: | Performed By (Initials) |
|---|---|---|---|---|---|---|
| | | | | | | |
| | | | | | | |
| | | | | | | |
| | | | | | | |
| | | | | | | |
| | | | | | | |
| | | | | | | |
| | | | | | | |
| | | | | | | |
| | | | | | | |
| | | | | | | |
| | | | | | | |
| | | | | | | |
| | | | | | | |
| | | | | | | |
| | | | | | | |
| | | | | | | |

# Yearly Maintenance Log

| Date | Smoke Detector Batteries | Carbon Monoxide Detector | Clean Gutters | Other: | Other: | Performed By (Initials) |
|------|--------------------------|--------------------------|---------------|--------|--------|-------------------------|
|      |                          |                          |               |        |        |                         |
|      |                          |                          |               |        |        |                         |
|      |                          |                          |               |        |        |                         |
|      |                          |                          |               |        |        |                         |
|      |                          |                          |               |        |        |                         |
|      |                          |                          |               |        |        |                         |
|      |                          |                          |               |        |        |                         |
|      |                          |                          |               |        |        |                         |
|      |                          |                          |               |        |        |                         |
|      |                          |                          |               |        |        |                         |
|      |                          |                          |               |        |        |                         |
|      |                          |                          |               |        |        |                         |
|      |                          |                          |               |        |        |                         |
|      |                          |                          |               |        |        |                         |
|      |                          |                          |               |        |        |                         |
|      |                          |                          |               |        |        |                         |
|      |                          |                          |               |        |        |                         |

# Notes

# Notes

# Notes

# Notes

# Systems Maintenance By Month

| JANUARY |
|---|
| Clean Pipes (Descale overnight) |
| Clean Showerheads and Taps |
| Clean and Recaulk Shower/Sinks |
| Clear Ice Dams In Gutters |
| |

| FEBRUARY |
|---|
| Deep Clean Oven and Stovetop |
| Clean Washer |
| Clean Dyer and Check Vent |
| Clean Dishwasher & Check Filter |
| |

| MARCH |
|---|
| Deep Spring Clean |
| Check Roof for Soft Spots |
| Check Sump Pump |
| Clean Gutters |
| |

# Systems Maintenance By Month

| APRIL |
|---|
| Spring Clean Kitchen |
| Vacuum HVAC Unit |
| Inspect Attic |
| Have AC Tuned |
| |

| MAY |
|---|
| Check Exhaust Fans |
| Check Ceiling Fan Blades/Dust |
| Check Weather Stripping |
| Fix Rust Spots |
| |

| JUNE |
|---|
| Clean Window Wells |
| Remove Dead Limbs From Trees |
| Touchup Paint |
| Remove Dead Plants From Flowerbeds |
| |

# Systems Maintenance By Month

| JULY |
|---|
| Clean/Stain Deck |
| Maintain Garage Door |
| Power Wash Concrete |
| Check Ductwork for Leaks |
| |

| AUGUST |
|---|
| Clean Garbage Disposal |
| Clean Out Freezer |
| Clean Window Treatments |
| Change Air Filters |
| |

| SEPTEMBER |
|---|
| Flush Water Heater |
| Furnace Tune-Up |
| Check Pantry for Expired Food |
| Check Carbon Monoxide Detectors |
| |

# Systems Maintenance By Month

| OCTOBER |
|---|
| Remove Exterior Hoses & Drain |
| Vacuum & Clean Furnace |
| Deep Clean Microwave |
| Winterize AC |
|  |

| NOVEMBER |
|---|
| Vacuum Fridge Coils |
| Deep Clean Fridge |
| Clean Fridge Drain Pan |
| Clean Circuit Breakers |
|  |

| DECEMBER |
|---|
| Test Electrical Outlets |
| Run Water in Unused Rooms |
| Inspect Fire Extinguishers |
| Replace Smoke Detector Batteries |
|  |

# Repairman Contact Information

Company Name:_____
Phone Number:_____
Email:_____
Technician Name:_____


Company Name:_____
Phone Number:_____
Email:_____
Technician Name:_____


Company Name:_____
Phone Number:_____
Email:_____
Technician Name:_____


Company Name:_____
Phone Number:_____
Email:_____
Technician Name:_____

# Repairman Contact Information

Company Name: _____
Phone Number: _____
Email: _____
Technician Name: _____


Company Name: _____
Phone Number: _____
Email: _____
Technician Name: _____


Company Name: _____
Phone Number: _____
Email: _____
Technician Name: _____


Company Name: _____
Phone Number: _____
Email: _____
Technician Name: _____

# Repairman Contact Information

Company Name: _____
Phone Number: _____
Email: _____
Technician Name: _____


Company Name: _____
Phone Number: _____
Email: _____
Technician Name: _____


Company Name: _____
Phone Number: _____
Email: _____
Technician Name: _____


Company Name: _____
Phone Number: _____
Email: _____
Technician Name: _____

# Home Warranty Information:

Company:_____

Premium Paid:_____

Contract Length:_____

Policy Number:_____

Customer Service Number:_____

Online Login User Name:_____

Online Login Password:_____

## Appliances Covered:

|   |                   |   |                  |
|---|-------------------|---|------------------|
|   | Refrigerator      |   | Ice Maker        |
|   | Stove             |   | Garbage Disposal |
|   | Washer            |   | Other            |
|   | Dryer             |   | Other            |
|   | Dishwasher        |   | Other            |
|   | Built-In Microwave|   | Other            |
|   | Trash Compactor   |   | Other            |

# Home Warranty Information (Continued):

## Systems Covered:

| | | | |
|---|---|---|---|
| | Air Conditioning | | Central Vac. |
| | Heating | | Septic Pump |
| | Electrical | | Well Pump |
| | Door Bell | | Other |
| | Smoke Detectors | | Other |
| | Ceiling Fans | | Other |
| | Water Heater | | Other |

## Usage Log:

| Date | What Was Serviced | Problem | Service Technician |
|---|---|---|---|
| | | | |
| | | | |
| | | | |
| | | | |
| | | | |
| | | | |
| | | | |

# Home Warranty Information (Continued):

| Date | What Was Serviced | Problem | Service Technician |
|---|---|---|---|
| | | | |
| | | | |
| | | | |
| | | | |
| | | | |
| | | | |
| | | | |
| | | | |
| | | | |
| | | | |
| | | | |
| | | | |
| | | | |
| | | | |
| | | | |
| | | | |

# Appliance Information

| Date of Purchase | Appliance | Purchased From | Price | Serial Number | Warranty |
|---|---|---|---|---|---|
| | | | | | |
| | | | | | |
| | | | | | |
| | | | | | |
| | | | | | |
| | | | | | |
| | | | | | |
| | | | | | |
| | | | | | |
| | | | | | |
| | | | | | |
| | | | | | |
| | | | | | |
| | | | | | |
| | | | | | |
| | | | | | |
| | | | | | |

# Appliance Information

| Date of Purchase | Appliance | Purchased From | Price | Serial Number | Warranty |
|---|---|---|---|---|---|
| | | | | | |
| | | | | | |
| | | | | | |
| | | | | | |
| | | | | | |
| | | | | | |
| | | | | | |
| | | | | | |
| | | | | | |
| | | | | | |
| | | | | | |
| | | | | | |
| | | | | | |
| | | | | | |
| | | | | | |
| | | | | | |
| | | | | | |
| | | | | | |

# Appliance Information

| Date of Purchase | Appliance | Purchased From | Price | Serial Number | Warranty |
|---|---|---|---|---|---|
|  |  |  |  |  |  |
|  |  |  |  |  |  |
|  |  |  |  |  |  |
|  |  |  |  |  |  |
|  |  |  |  |  |  |
|  |  |  |  |  |  |
|  |  |  |  |  |  |
|  |  |  |  |  |  |
|  |  |  |  |  |  |
|  |  |  |  |  |  |
|  |  |  |  |  |  |
|  |  |  |  |  |  |
|  |  |  |  |  |  |
|  |  |  |  |  |  |
|  |  |  |  |  |  |
|  |  |  |  |  |  |
|  |  |  |  |  |  |

# Appliance Repair Log

| Date of Service | Appliance | Repairman | Contact Info | Cost | Warranty |
|---|---|---|---|---|---|
| | | | | | |
| | | | | | |
| | | | | | |
| | | | | | |
| | | | | | |
| | | | | | |
| | | | | | |
| | | | | | |
| | | | | | |
| | | | | | |
| | | | | | |
| | | | | | |
| | | | | | |
| | | | | | |
| | | | | | |
| | | | | | |
| | | | | | |

# Appliance Repair Log

| Date of Service | Appliance | Repairman | Contact Info | Cost | Warranty |
|---|---|---|---|---|---|
| | | | | | |
| | | | | | |
| | | | | | |
| | | | | | |
| | | | | | |
| | | | | | |
| | | | | | |
| | | | | | |
| | | | | | |
| | | | | | |
| | | | | | |
| | | | | | |
| | | | | | |
| | | | | | |
| | | | | | |
| | | | | | |
| | | | | | |
| | | | | | |

# Appliance Repair Log

| Date of Service | Appliance | Repairman | Contact Info | Cost | Warranty |
|---|---|---|---|---|---|
| | | | | | |
| | | | | | |
| | | | | | |
| | | | | | |
| | | | | | |
| | | | | | |
| | | | | | |
| | | | | | |
| | | | | | |
| | | | | | |
| | | | | | |
| | | | | | |
| | | | | | |
| | | | | | |
| | | | | | |
| | | | | | |
| | | | | | |
| | | | | | |

# Monthly Maintenance Log

| Date | Check Smoke Detectors | Change Furnace Filter | Other: | Other: | Performed By (Initials) |
|------|----------------------|----------------------|--------|--------|------------------------|
|      |                      |                      |        |        |                        |
|      |                      |                      |        |        |                        |
|      |                      |                      |        |        |                        |
|      |                      |                      |        |        |                        |
|      |                      |                      |        |        |                        |
|      |                      |                      |        |        |                        |
|      |                      |                      |        |        |                        |
|      |                      |                      |        |        |                        |
|      |                      |                      |        |        |                        |
|      |                      |                      |        |        |                        |
|      |                      |                      |        |        |                        |
|      |                      |                      |        |        |                        |
|      |                      |                      |        |        |                        |
|      |                      |                      |        |        |                        |
|      |                      |                      |        |        |                        |
|      |                      |                      |        |        |                        |
|      |                      |                      |        |        |                        |

# Monthly Maintenance Log

| Date | Check Smoke Detectors | Change Furnace Filter | Other: | Other: | Performed By (Initials) |
|------|----------------------|----------------------|--------|--------|------------------------|
|      |                      |                      |        |        |                        |
|      |                      |                      |        |        |                        |
|      |                      |                      |        |        |                        |
|      |                      |                      |        |        |                        |
|      |                      |                      |        |        |                        |
|      |                      |                      |        |        |                        |
|      |                      |                      |        |        |                        |
|      |                      |                      |        |        |                        |
|      |                      |                      |        |        |                        |
|      |                      |                      |        |        |                        |
|      |                      |                      |        |        |                        |
|      |                      |                      |        |        |                        |
|      |                      |                      |        |        |                        |
|      |                      |                      |        |        |                        |
|      |                      |                      |        |        |                        |
|      |                      |                      |        |        |                        |
|      |                      |                      |        |        |                        |

# Monthly Maintenance Log

| Date | Check Smoke Detectors | Change Furnace Filter | Other: | Other: | Performed By (Initials) |
|---|---|---|---|---|---|
| | | | | | |
| | | | | | |
| | | | | | |
| | | | | | |
| | | | | | |
| | | | | | |
| | | | | | |
| | | | | | |
| | | | | | |
| | | | | | |
| | | | | | |
| | | | | | |
| | | | | | |
| | | | | | |
| | | | | | |
| | | | | | |
| | | | | | |
| | | | | | |

# Quarterly Maintenance Log

| Date | Check Basement/Crawl Space For Leaks | Clean Fridge | Clean Baseboards | Check Shower/Sink Drain Issues | Performed By (Initials) |
|---|---|---|---|---|---|
|  |  |  |  |  |  |
|  |  |  |  |  |  |
|  |  |  |  |  |  |
|  |  |  |  |  |  |
|  |  |  |  |  |  |
|  |  |  |  |  |  |
|  |  |  |  |  |  |
|  |  |  |  |  |  |
|  |  |  |  |  |  |
|  |  |  |  |  |  |
|  |  |  |  |  |  |
|  |  |  |  |  |  |
|  |  |  |  |  |  |
|  |  |  |  |  |  |
|  |  |  |  |  |  |
|  |  |  |  |  |  |
|  |  |  |  |  |  |
|  |  |  |  |  |  |

# Quarterly Maintenance Log

| Date | Check Basement/Crawl Space For Leaks | Clean Fridge | Clean Baseboards | Check Shower/Sink Drain Issues | Performed By (Initials) |
|------|--------------------------------------|--------------|------------------|-------------------------------|-------------------------|
|      |                                      |              |                  |                               |                         |
|      |                                      |              |                  |                               |                         |
|      |                                      |              |                  |                               |                         |
|      |                                      |              |                  |                               |                         |
|      |                                      |              |                  |                               |                         |
|      |                                      |              |                  |                               |                         |
|      |                                      |              |                  |                               |                         |
|      |                                      |              |                  |                               |                         |
|      |                                      |              |                  |                               |                         |
|      |                                      |              |                  |                               |                         |
|      |                                      |              |                  |                               |                         |
|      |                                      |              |                  |                               |                         |
|      |                                      |              |                  |                               |                         |
|      |                                      |              |                  |                               |                         |
|      |                                      |              |                  |                               |                         |
|      |                                      |              |                  |                               |                         |
|      |                                      |              |                  |                               |                         |

# Quarterly Maintenance Log

| Date | Check Basement/Crawl Space For Leaks | Clean Fridge | Clean Baseboards | Check Shower/Sink Drain Issues | Performed By (Initials) |
|---|---|---|---|---|---|
| | | | | | |
| | | | | | |
| | | | | | |
| | | | | | |
| | | | | | |
| | | | | | |
| | | | | | |
| | | | | | |
| | | | | | |
| | | | | | |
| | | | | | |
| | | | | | |
| | | | | | |
| | | | | | |
| | | | | | |
| | | | | | |
| | | | | | |

# Yearly Maintenance Log

| Date | Smoke Detector Batteries | Carbon Monoxide Detector | Clean Gutters | Other: | Other: | Performed By (Initials) |
|------|--------------------------|--------------------------|---------------|--------|--------|-------------------------|
|      |                          |                          |               |        |        |                         |
|      |                          |                          |               |        |        |                         |
|      |                          |                          |               |        |        |                         |
|      |                          |                          |               |        |        |                         |
|      |                          |                          |               |        |        |                         |
|      |                          |                          |               |        |        |                         |
|      |                          |                          |               |        |        |                         |
|      |                          |                          |               |        |        |                         |
|      |                          |                          |               |        |        |                         |
|      |                          |                          |               |        |        |                         |
|      |                          |                          |               |        |        |                         |
|      |                          |                          |               |        |        |                         |
|      |                          |                          |               |        |        |                         |
|      |                          |                          |               |        |        |                         |
|      |                          |                          |               |        |        |                         |
|      |                          |                          |               |        |        |                         |
|      |                          |                          |               |        |        |                         |
|      |                          |                          |               |        |        |                         |

# Yearly Maintenance Log

| Date | Smoke Detector Batteries | Carbon Monoxide Detector | Clean Gutters | Other: | Other: | Performed By (Initials) |
|------|--------------------------|--------------------------|---------------|--------|--------|-------------------------|
|      |                          |                          |               |        |        |                         |
|      |                          |                          |               |        |        |                         |
|      |                          |                          |               |        |        |                         |
|      |                          |                          |               |        |        |                         |
|      |                          |                          |               |        |        |                         |
|      |                          |                          |               |        |        |                         |
|      |                          |                          |               |        |        |                         |
|      |                          |                          |               |        |        |                         |
|      |                          |                          |               |        |        |                         |
|      |                          |                          |               |        |        |                         |
|      |                          |                          |               |        |        |                         |
|      |                          |                          |               |        |        |                         |
|      |                          |                          |               |        |        |                         |
|      |                          |                          |               |        |        |                         |
|      |                          |                          |               |        |        |                         |
|      |                          |                          |               |        |        |                         |
|      |                          |                          |               |        |        |                         |

# Yearly Maintenance Log

| Date | Smoke Detector Batteries | Carbon Monoxide Detector | Clean Gutters | Other: | Other: | Performed By (Initials) |
|------|--------------------------|--------------------------|---------------|--------|--------|-------------------------|
|      |                          |                          |               |        |        |                         |
|      |                          |                          |               |        |        |                         |
|      |                          |                          |               |        |        |                         |
|      |                          |                          |               |        |        |                         |
|      |                          |                          |               |        |        |                         |
|      |                          |                          |               |        |        |                         |
|      |                          |                          |               |        |        |                         |
|      |                          |                          |               |        |        |                         |
|      |                          |                          |               |        |        |                         |
|      |                          |                          |               |        |        |                         |
|      |                          |                          |               |        |        |                         |
|      |                          |                          |               |        |        |                         |
|      |                          |                          |               |        |        |                         |
|      |                          |                          |               |        |        |                         |
|      |                          |                          |               |        |        |                         |
|      |                          |                          |               |        |        |                         |
|      |                          |                          |               |        |        |                         |

# Notes

# Notes

# Notes

# Notes

# Systems Maintenance By Month

| JANUARY |
| --- |
| Clean Pipes (Descale overnight) |
| Clean Showerheads and Taps |
| Clean and Recaulk Shower/Sinks |
| Clear Ice Dams In Gutters |
|  |

| FEBRUARY |
| --- |
| Deep Clean Oven and Stovetop |
| Clean Washer |
| Clean Dyer and Check Vent |
| Clean Dishwasher & Check Filter |
|  |

| MARCH |
| --- |
| Deep Spring Clean |
| Check Roof for Soft Spots |
| Check Sump Pump |
| Clean Gutters |
|  |

# Systems Maintenance By Month

| APRIL |
|---|
| Spring Clean Kitchen |
| Vacuum HVAC Unit |
| Inspect Attic |
| Have AC Tuned |
|  |

| MAY |
|---|
| Check Exhaust Fans |
| Check Ceiling Fan Blades/Dust |
| Check Weather Stripping |
| Fix Rust Spots |
|  |

| JUNE |
|---|
| Clean Window Wells |
| Remove Dead Limbs From Trees |
| Touchup Paint |
| Remove Dead Plants From Flowerbeds |
|  |

# Systems Maintenance By Month

| JULY |
| --- |
| Clean/Stain Deck |
| Maintain Garage Door |
| Power Wash Concrete |
| Check Ductwork for Leaks |
| |

| AUGUST |
| --- |
| Clean Garbage Disposal |
| Clean Out Freezer |
| Clean Window Treatments |
| Change Air Filters |
| |

| SEPTEMBER |
| --- |
| Flush Water Heater |
| Furnace Tune-Up |
| Check Pantry for Expired Food |
| Check Carbon Monoxide Detectors |
| |

# Systems Maintenance By Month

| OCTOBER |
|---|
| Remove Exterior Hoses & Drain |
| Vacuum & Clean Furnace |
| Deep Clean Microwave |
| Winterize AC |
|  |

| NOVEMBER |
|---|
| Vacuum Fridge Coils |
| Deep Clean Fridge |
| Clean Fridge Drain Pan |
| Clean Circuit Breakers |
|  |

| DECEMBER |
|---|
| Test Electrical Outlets |
| Run Water in Unused Rooms |
| Inspect Fire Extinguishers |
| Replace Smoke Detector Batteries |
|  |

# Repairman Contact Information

Company Name: _____
Phone Number: _____
Email: _____
Technician Name: _____


Company Name: _____
Phone Number: _____
Email: _____
Technician Name: _____


Company Name: _____
Phone Number: _____
Email: _____
Technician Name: _____


Company Name: _____
Phone Number: _____
Email: _____
Technician Name: _____

# Repairman Contact Information

Company Name: _____
Phone Number: _____
Email: _____
Technician Name: _____


Company Name: _____
Phone Number: _____
Email: _____
Technician Name: _____


Company Name: _____
Phone Number: _____
Email: _____
Technician Name: _____


Company Name: _____
Phone Number: _____
Email: _____
Technician Name: _____

# Repairman Contact Information

Company Name:_____
Phone Number:_____
Email:_____
Technician Name:_____


Company Name:_____
Phone Number:_____
Email:_____
Technician Name:_____


Company Name:_____
Phone Number:_____
Email:_____
Technician Name:_____


Company Name:_____
Phone Number:_____
Email:_____
Technician Name:_____

# Home Warranty Information:

Company:_____

Premium Paid:_____

Contract Length:_____

Policy Number:_____

Customer Service Number:_____

Online Login User Name:_____

Online Login Password:_____

## Appliances Covered:

| | | | |
|---|---|---|---|
| | Refrigerator | | Ice Maker |
| | Stove | | Garbage Disposal |
| | Washer | | Other |
| | Dryer | | Other |
| | Dishwasher | | Other |
| | Built-In Microwave | | Other |
| | Trash Compactor | | Other |

# Home Warranty Information (Continued):

## Systems Covered:

| | | | | |
|---|---|---|---|---|
| | Air Conditioning | | | Central Vac. |
| | Heating | | | Septic Pump |
| | Electrical | | | Well Pump |
| | Door Bell | | | Other |
| | Smoke Detectors | | | Other |
| | Ceiling Fans | | | Other |
| | Water Heater | | | Other |

## Usage Log:

| Date | What Was Serviced | Problem | Service Technician |
|---|---|---|---|
| | | | |
| | | | |
| | | | |
| | | | |
| | | | |
| | | | |
| | | | |

# Home Warranty Information (Continued):

| Date | What Was Serviced | Problem | Service Technician |
|------|-------------------|---------|--------------------|
|      |                   |         |                    |
|      |                   |         |                    |
|      |                   |         |                    |
|      |                   |         |                    |
|      |                   |         |                    |
|      |                   |         |                    |
|      |                   |         |                    |
|      |                   |         |                    |
|      |                   |         |                    |
|      |                   |         |                    |
|      |                   |         |                    |
|      |                   |         |                    |
|      |                   |         |                    |
|      |                   |         |                    |
|      |                   |         |                    |
|      |                   |         |                    |

# Appliance Information

| Date of Purchase | Appliance | Purchased From | Price | Serial Number | Warranty |
|---|---|---|---|---|---|
| | | | | | |
| | | | | | |
| | | | | | |
| | | | | | |
| | | | | | |
| | | | | | |
| | | | | | |
| | | | | | |
| | | | | | |
| | | | | | |
| | | | | | |
| | | | | | |
| | | | | | |
| | | | | | |
| | | | | | |
| | | | | | |
| | | | | | |
| | | | | | |

# Appliance Information

| Date of Purchase | Appliance | Purchased From | Price | Serial Number | Warranty |
|---|---|---|---|---|---|
| | | | | | |
| | | | | | |
| | | | | | |
| | | | | | |
| | | | | | |
| | | | | | |
| | | | | | |
| | | | | | |
| | | | | | |
| | | | | | |
| | | | | | |
| | | | | | |
| | | | | | |
| | | | | | |
| | | | | | |
| | | | | | |
| | | | | | |

# Appliance Information

| Date of Purchase | Appliance | Purchased From | Price | Serial Number | Warranty |
|---|---|---|---|---|---|
| | | | | | |
| | | | | | |
| | | | | | |
| | | | | | |
| | | | | | |
| | | | | | |
| | | | | | |
| | | | | | |
| | | | | | |
| | | | | | |
| | | | | | |
| | | | | | |
| | | | | | |
| | | | | | |
| | | | | | |
| | | | | | |
| | | | | | |

# Appliance Repair Log

| Date of Service | Appliance | Repairman | Contact Info | Cost | Warranty |
|---|---|---|---|---|---|
| | | | | | |
| | | | | | |
| | | | | | |
| | | | | | |
| | | | | | |
| | | | | | |
| | | | | | |
| | | | | | |
| | | | | | |
| | | | | | |
| | | | | | |
| | | | | | |
| | | | | | |
| | | | | | |
| | | | | | |
| | | | | | |
| | | | | | |
| | | | | | |

# Appliance Repair Log

| Date of Service | Appliance | Repairman | Contact Info | Cost | Warranty |
|---|---|---|---|---|---|
| | | | | | |
| | | | | | |
| | | | | | |
| | | | | | |
| | | | | | |
| | | | | | |
| | | | | | |
| | | | | | |
| | | | | | |
| | | | | | |
| | | | | | |
| | | | | | |
| | | | | | |
| | | | | | |
| | | | | | |
| | | | | | |
| | | | | | |

# Appliance Repair Log

| Date of Service | Appliance | Repairman | Contact Info | Cost | Warranty |
|---|---|---|---|---|---|
| | | | | | |
| | | | | | |
| | | | | | |
| | | | | | |
| | | | | | |
| | | | | | |
| | | | | | |
| | | | | | |
| | | | | | |
| | | | | | |
| | | | | | |
| | | | | | |
| | | | | | |
| | | | | | |
| | | | | | |
| | | | | | |
| | | | | | |

# Monthly Maintenance Log

| Date | Check Smoke Detectors | Change Furnace Filter | Other: | Other: | Performed By (Initials) |
|------|----------------------|----------------------|--------|--------|------------------------|
|      |                      |                      |        |        |                        |
|      |                      |                      |        |        |                        |
|      |                      |                      |        |        |                        |
|      |                      |                      |        |        |                        |
|      |                      |                      |        |        |                        |
|      |                      |                      |        |        |                        |
|      |                      |                      |        |        |                        |
|      |                      |                      |        |        |                        |
|      |                      |                      |        |        |                        |
|      |                      |                      |        |        |                        |
|      |                      |                      |        |        |                        |
|      |                      |                      |        |        |                        |
|      |                      |                      |        |        |                        |
|      |                      |                      |        |        |                        |
|      |                      |                      |        |        |                        |
|      |                      |                      |        |        |                        |
|      |                      |                      |        |        |                        |
|      |                      |                      |        |        |                        |

# Monthly Maintenance Log

| Date | Check Smoke Detectors | Change Furnace Filter | Other: | Other: | Performed By (Initials) |
|---|---|---|---|---|---|
| | | | | | |
| | | | | | |
| | | | | | |
| | | | | | |
| | | | | | |
| | | | | | |
| | | | | | |
| | | | | | |
| | | | | | |
| | | | | | |
| | | | | | |
| | | | | | |
| | | | | | |
| | | | | | |
| | | | | | |
| | | | | | |
| | | | | | |
| | | | | | |

# Monthly Maintenance Log

| Date | Check Smoke Detectors | Change Furnace Filter | Other: | Other: | Performed By (Initials) |
|---|---|---|---|---|---|
| | | | | | |
| | | | | | |
| | | | | | |
| | | | | | |
| | | | | | |
| | | | | | |
| | | | | | |
| | | | | | |
| | | | | | |
| | | | | | |
| | | | | | |
| | | | | | |
| | | | | | |
| | | | | | |
| | | | | | |
| | | | | | |
| | | | | | |
| | | | | | |

# Quarterly Maintenance Log

| Date | Check Basement/Crawl Space For Leaks | Clean Fridge | Clean Baseboards | Check Shower/Sink Drain Issues | Performed By (Initials) |
|------|--------------------------------------|--------------|------------------|--------------------------------|-------------------------|
|      |                                      |              |                  |                                |                         |
|      |                                      |              |                  |                                |                         |
|      |                                      |              |                  |                                |                         |
|      |                                      |              |                  |                                |                         |
|      |                                      |              |                  |                                |                         |
|      |                                      |              |                  |                                |                         |
|      |                                      |              |                  |                                |                         |
|      |                                      |              |                  |                                |                         |
|      |                                      |              |                  |                                |                         |
|      |                                      |              |                  |                                |                         |
|      |                                      |              |                  |                                |                         |
|      |                                      |              |                  |                                |                         |
|      |                                      |              |                  |                                |                         |
|      |                                      |              |                  |                                |                         |
|      |                                      |              |                  |                                |                         |
|      |                                      |              |                  |                                |                         |
|      |                                      |              |                  |                                |                         |

# Quarterly Maintenance Log

| Date | Check Basement/Crawl Space For Leaks | Clean Fridge | Clean Baseboards | Check Shower/Sink Drain Issues | Performed By (Initials) |
|---|---|---|---|---|---|
|  |  |  |  |  |  |
|  |  |  |  |  |  |
|  |  |  |  |  |  |
|  |  |  |  |  |  |
|  |  |  |  |  |  |
|  |  |  |  |  |  |
|  |  |  |  |  |  |
|  |  |  |  |  |  |
|  |  |  |  |  |  |
|  |  |  |  |  |  |
|  |  |  |  |  |  |
|  |  |  |  |  |  |
|  |  |  |  |  |  |
|  |  |  |  |  |  |
|  |  |  |  |  |  |
|  |  |  |  |  |  |
|  |  |  |  |  |  |
|  |  |  |  |  |  |

# Quarterly Maintenance Log

| Date | Check Basement/Crawl Space For Leaks | Clean Fridge | Clean Baseboards | Check Shower/Sink Drain Issues | Performed By (Initials) |
|------|---------------------------------------|--------------|------------------|-------------------------------|--------------------------|
|      |                                       |              |                  |                               |                          |
|      |                                       |              |                  |                               |                          |
|      |                                       |              |                  |                               |                          |
|      |                                       |              |                  |                               |                          |
|      |                                       |              |                  |                               |                          |
|      |                                       |              |                  |                               |                          |
|      |                                       |              |                  |                               |                          |
|      |                                       |              |                  |                               |                          |
|      |                                       |              |                  |                               |                          |
|      |                                       |              |                  |                               |                          |
|      |                                       |              |                  |                               |                          |
|      |                                       |              |                  |                               |                          |
|      |                                       |              |                  |                               |                          |
|      |                                       |              |                  |                               |                          |
|      |                                       |              |                  |                               |                          |
|      |                                       |              |                  |                               |                          |
|      |                                       |              |                  |                               |                          |

# Yearly Maintenance Log

| Date | Smoke Detector Batteries | Carbon Monoxide Detector | Clean Gutters | Other: | Other: | Performed By (Initials) |
|------|--------------------------|--------------------------|---------------|--------|--------|-------------------------|
|      |                          |                          |               |        |        |                         |
|      |                          |                          |               |        |        |                         |
|      |                          |                          |               |        |        |                         |
|      |                          |                          |               |        |        |                         |
|      |                          |                          |               |        |        |                         |
|      |                          |                          |               |        |        |                         |
|      |                          |                          |               |        |        |                         |
|      |                          |                          |               |        |        |                         |
|      |                          |                          |               |        |        |                         |
|      |                          |                          |               |        |        |                         |
|      |                          |                          |               |        |        |                         |
|      |                          |                          |               |        |        |                         |
|      |                          |                          |               |        |        |                         |
|      |                          |                          |               |        |        |                         |
|      |                          |                          |               |        |        |                         |
|      |                          |                          |               |        |        |                         |
|      |                          |                          |               |        |        |                         |
|      |                          |                          |               |        |        |                         |

# Yearly Maintenance Log

| Date | Smoke Detector Batteries | Carbon Monoxide Detector | Clean Gutters | Other: | Other: | Performed By (Initials) |
|------|--------------------------|--------------------------|---------------|--------|--------|-------------------------|
|      |                          |                          |               |        |        |                         |
|      |                          |                          |               |        |        |                         |
|      |                          |                          |               |        |        |                         |
|      |                          |                          |               |        |        |                         |
|      |                          |                          |               |        |        |                         |
|      |                          |                          |               |        |        |                         |
|      |                          |                          |               |        |        |                         |
|      |                          |                          |               |        |        |                         |
|      |                          |                          |               |        |        |                         |
|      |                          |                          |               |        |        |                         |
|      |                          |                          |               |        |        |                         |
|      |                          |                          |               |        |        |                         |
|      |                          |                          |               |        |        |                         |
|      |                          |                          |               |        |        |                         |
|      |                          |                          |               |        |        |                         |
|      |                          |                          |               |        |        |                         |
|      |                          |                          |               |        |        |                         |

# Yearly Maintenance Log

| Date | Smoke Detector Batteries | Carbon Monoxide Detector | Clean Gutters | Other: | Other: | Performed By (Initials) |
|------|--------------------------|--------------------------|---------------|--------|--------|-------------------------|
|      |                          |                          |               |        |        |                         |
|      |                          |                          |               |        |        |                         |
|      |                          |                          |               |        |        |                         |
|      |                          |                          |               |        |        |                         |
|      |                          |                          |               |        |        |                         |
|      |                          |                          |               |        |        |                         |
|      |                          |                          |               |        |        |                         |
|      |                          |                          |               |        |        |                         |
|      |                          |                          |               |        |        |                         |
|      |                          |                          |               |        |        |                         |
|      |                          |                          |               |        |        |                         |
|      |                          |                          |               |        |        |                         |
|      |                          |                          |               |        |        |                         |
|      |                          |                          |               |        |        |                         |
|      |                          |                          |               |        |        |                         |
|      |                          |                          |               |        |        |                         |
|      |                          |                          |               |        |        |                         |

# Notes

# Notes

# Notes

# Notes

# Systems Maintenance By Month

| JANUARY |
| --- |
| Clean Pipes (Descale overnight) |
| Clean Showerheads and Taps |
| Clean and Recaulk Shower/Sinks |
| Clear Ice Dams In Gutters |
| |

| FEBRUARY |
| --- |
| Deep Clean Oven and Stovetop |
| Clean Washer |
| Clean Dyer and Check Vent |
| Clean Dishwasher & Check Filter |
| |

| MARCH |
| --- |
| Deep Spring Clean |
| Check Roof for Soft Spots |
| Check Sump Pump |
| Clean Gutters |
| |

# Systems Maintenance By Month

| APRIL |
|---|
| Spring Clean Kitchen |
| Vacuum HVAC Unit |
| Inspect Attic |
| Have AC Tuned |
|  |

| MAY |
|---|
| Check Exhaust Fans |
| Check Ceiling Fan Blades/Dust |
| Check Weather Stripping |
| Fix Rust Spots |
|  |

| JUNE |
|---|
| Clean Window Wells |
| Remove Dead Limbs From Trees |
| Touchup Paint |
| Remove Dead Plants From Flowerbeds |
|  |

# Systems Maintenance By Month

### JULY

| |
|---|
| Clean/Stain Deck |
| Maintain Garage Door |
| Power Wash Concrete |
| Check Ductwork for Leaks |
| |

### AUGUST

| |
|---|
| Clean Garbage Disposal |
| Clean Out Freezer |
| Clean Window Treatments |
| Change Air Filters |
| |

### SEPTEMBER

| |
|---|
| Flush Water Heater |
| Furnace Tune-Up |
| Check Pantry for Expired Food |
| Check Carbon Monoxide Detectors |
| |

# Systems Maintenance By Month

| OCTOBER |
| --- |
| Remove Exterior Hoses & Drain |
| Vacuum & Clean Furnace |
| Deep Clean Microwave |
| Winterize AC |
| |

| NOVEMBER |
| --- |
| Vacuum Fridge Coils |
| Deep Clean Fridge |
| Clean Fridge Drain Pan |
| Clean Circuit Breakers |
| |

| DECEMBER |
| --- |
| Test Electrical Outlets |
| Run Water in Unused Rooms |
| Inspect Fire Extinguishers |
| Replace Smoke Detector Batteries |
| |

# Repairman Contact Information

Company Name: _____
Phone Number: _____
Email: _____
Technician Name: _____


Company Name: _____
Phone Number: _____
Email: _____
Technician Name: _____


Company Name: _____
Phone Number: _____
Email: _____
Technician Name: _____


Company Name: _____
Phone Number: _____
Email: _____
Technician Name: _____

# Repairman Contact Information

Company Name: _____
Phone Number: _____
Email: _____
Technician Name: _____


Company Name: _____
Phone Number: _____
Email: _____
Technician Name: _____


Company Name: _____
Phone Number: _____
Email: _____
Technician Name: _____


Company Name: _____
Phone Number: _____
Email: _____
Technician Name: _____

# Repairman Contact Information

Company Name: _____
Phone Number: _____
Email: _____
Technician Name: _____


Company Name: _____
Phone Number: _____
Email: _____
Technician Name: _____


Company Name: _____
Phone Number: _____
Email: _____
Technician Name: _____


Company Name: _____
Phone Number: _____
Email: _____
Technician Name: _____

# Home Warranty Information:

Company:_____

Premium Paid:_____

Contract Length:_____

Policy Number:_____

Customer Service Number:_____

Online Login User Name:_____

Online Login Password:_____

## Appliances Covered:

|  |  |
|---|---|
| Refrigerator | Ice Maker |
| Stove | Garbage Disposal |
| Washer | Other |
| Dryer | Other |
| Dishwasher | Other |
| Built-In Microwave | Other |
| Trash Compactor | Other |

# Home Warranty Information (Continued):

## Systems Covered:

| | | | |
|---|---|---|---|
| | Air Conditioning | | Central Vac. |
| | Heating | | Septic Pump |
| | Electrical | | Well Pump |
| | Door Bell | | Other |
| | Smoke Detectors | | Other |
| | Ceiling Fans | | Other |
| | Water Heater | | Other |

## Usage Log:

| Date | What Was Serviced | Problem | Service Technician |
|---|---|---|---|
| | | | |
| | | | |
| | | | |
| | | | |
| | | | |
| | | | |
| | | | |

# Home Warranty Information (Continued):

| Date | What Was Serviced | Problem | Service Technician |
|------|-------------------|---------|--------------------|
|      |                   |         |                    |
|      |                   |         |                    |
|      |                   |         |                    |
|      |                   |         |                    |
|      |                   |         |                    |
|      |                   |         |                    |
|      |                   |         |                    |
|      |                   |         |                    |
|      |                   |         |                    |
|      |                   |         |                    |
|      |                   |         |                    |
|      |                   |         |                    |
|      |                   |         |                    |
|      |                   |         |                    |
|      |                   |         |                    |
|      |                   |         |                    |

# Appliance Information

| Date of Purchase | Appliance | Purchased From | Price | Serial Number | Warranty |
|---|---|---|---|---|---|
| | | | | | |
| | | | | | |
| | | | | | |
| | | | | | |
| | | | | | |
| | | | | | |
| | | | | | |
| | | | | | |
| | | | | | |
| | | | | | |
| | | | | | |
| | | | | | |
| | | | | | |
| | | | | | |
| | | | | | |
| | | | | | |
| | | | | | |

# Appliance Information

| Date of Purchase | Appliance | Purchased From | Price | Serial Number | Warranty |
|---|---|---|---|---|---|
| | | | | | |
| | | | | | |
| | | | | | |
| | | | | | |
| | | | | | |
| | | | | | |
| | | | | | |
| | | | | | |
| | | | | | |
| | | | | | |
| | | | | | |
| | | | | | |
| | | | | | |
| | | | | | |
| | | | | | |
| | | | | | |
| | | | | | |

# Appliance Information

| Date of Purchase | Appliance | Purchased From | Price | Serial Number | Warranty |
|---|---|---|---|---|---|
| | | | | | |
| | | | | | |
| | | | | | |
| | | | | | |
| | | | | | |
| | | | | | |
| | | | | | |
| | | | | | |
| | | | | | |
| | | | | | |
| | | | | | |
| | | | | | |
| | | | | | |
| | | | | | |
| | | | | | |
| | | | | | |
| | | | | | |

# Appliance Repair Log

| Date of Service | Appliance | Repairman | Contact Info | Cost | Warranty |
|---|---|---|---|---|---|
| | | | | | |
| | | | | | |
| | | | | | |
| | | | | | |
| | | | | | |
| | | | | | |
| | | | | | |
| | | | | | |
| | | | | | |
| | | | | | |
| | | | | | |
| | | | | | |
| | | | | | |
| | | | | | |
| | | | | | |
| | | | | | |
| | | | | | |

# Appliance Repair Log

| Date of Service | Appliance | Repairman | Contact Info | Cost | Warranty |
|---|---|---|---|---|---|
| | | | | | |
| | | | | | |
| | | | | | |
| | | | | | |
| | | | | | |
| | | | | | |
| | | | | | |
| | | | | | |
| | | | | | |
| | | | | | |
| | | | | | |
| | | | | | |
| | | | | | |
| | | | | | |
| | | | | | |
| | | | | | |
| | | | | | |

# Appliance Repair Log

| Date of Service | Appliance | Repairman | Contact Info | Cost | Warranty |
|---|---|---|---|---|---|
| | | | | | |
| | | | | | |
| | | | | | |
| | | | | | |
| | | | | | |
| | | | | | |
| | | | | | |
| | | | | | |
| | | | | | |
| | | | | | |
| | | | | | |
| | | | | | |
| | | | | | |
| | | | | | |
| | | | | | |
| | | | | | |
| | | | | | |

# Monthly Maintenance Log

| Date | Check Smoke Detectors | Change Furnace Filter | Other: | Other: | Performed By (Initials) |
|------|----------------------|----------------------|--------|--------|-------------------------|
|      |                      |                      |        |        |                         |
|      |                      |                      |        |        |                         |
|      |                      |                      |        |        |                         |
|      |                      |                      |        |        |                         |
|      |                      |                      |        |        |                         |
|      |                      |                      |        |        |                         |
|      |                      |                      |        |        |                         |
|      |                      |                      |        |        |                         |
|      |                      |                      |        |        |                         |
|      |                      |                      |        |        |                         |
|      |                      |                      |        |        |                         |
|      |                      |                      |        |        |                         |
|      |                      |                      |        |        |                         |
|      |                      |                      |        |        |                         |
|      |                      |                      |        |        |                         |
|      |                      |                      |        |        |                         |
|      |                      |                      |        |        |                         |

# Monthly Maintenance Log

| Date | Check Smoke Detectors | Change Furnace Filter | Other: | Other: | Performed By (Initials) |
|------|----------------------|----------------------|--------|--------|------------------------|
|      |                      |                      |        |        |                        |
|      |                      |                      |        |        |                        |
|      |                      |                      |        |        |                        |
|      |                      |                      |        |        |                        |
|      |                      |                      |        |        |                        |
|      |                      |                      |        |        |                        |
|      |                      |                      |        |        |                        |
|      |                      |                      |        |        |                        |
|      |                      |                      |        |        |                        |
|      |                      |                      |        |        |                        |
|      |                      |                      |        |        |                        |
|      |                      |                      |        |        |                        |
|      |                      |                      |        |        |                        |
|      |                      |                      |        |        |                        |
|      |                      |                      |        |        |                        |
|      |                      |                      |        |        |                        |
|      |                      |                      |        |        |                        |

# Monthly Maintenance Log

| Date | Check Smoke Detectors | Change Furnace Filter | Other: | Other: | Performed By (Initials) |
|------|----------------------|----------------------|--------|--------|------------------------|
|      |                      |                      |        |        |                        |
|      |                      |                      |        |        |                        |
|      |                      |                      |        |        |                        |
|      |                      |                      |        |        |                        |
|      |                      |                      |        |        |                        |
|      |                      |                      |        |        |                        |
|      |                      |                      |        |        |                        |
|      |                      |                      |        |        |                        |
|      |                      |                      |        |        |                        |
|      |                      |                      |        |        |                        |
|      |                      |                      |        |        |                        |
|      |                      |                      |        |        |                        |
|      |                      |                      |        |        |                        |
|      |                      |                      |        |        |                        |
|      |                      |                      |        |        |                        |
|      |                      |                      |        |        |                        |
|      |                      |                      |        |        |                        |

# Quarterly Maintenance Log

| Date | Check Basement/Crawl Space For Leaks | Clean Fridge | Clean Baseboards | Check Shower/Sink Drain Issues | Performed By (Initials) |
|---|---|---|---|---|---|
| | | | | | |
| | | | | | |
| | | | | | |
| | | | | | |
| | | | | | |
| | | | | | |
| | | | | | |
| | | | | | |
| | | | | | |
| | | | | | |
| | | | | | |
| | | | | | |
| | | | | | |
| | | | | | |
| | | | | | |
| | | | | | |
| | | | | | |

# Quarterly Maintenance Log

| Date | Check Basement/Crawl Space For Leaks | Clean Fridge | Clean Baseboards | Check Shower/Sink Drain Issues | Performed By (Initials) |
|---|---|---|---|---|---|
| | | | | | |
| | | | | | |
| | | | | | |
| | | | | | |
| | | | | | |
| | | | | | |
| | | | | | |
| | | | | | |
| | | | | | |
| | | | | | |
| | | | | | |
| | | | | | |
| | | | | | |
| | | | | | |
| | | | | | |
| | | | | | |
| | | | | | |
| | | | | | |

# Quarterly Maintenance Log

| Date | Check Basement/Crawl Space For Leaks | Clean Fridge | Clean Baseboards | Check Shower/Sink Drain Issues | Performed By (Initials) |
|------|--------------------------------------|--------------|------------------|--------------------------------|--------------------------|
|      |                                      |              |                  |                                |                          |
|      |                                      |              |                  |                                |                          |
|      |                                      |              |                  |                                |                          |
|      |                                      |              |                  |                                |                          |
|      |                                      |              |                  |                                |                          |
|      |                                      |              |                  |                                |                          |
|      |                                      |              |                  |                                |                          |
|      |                                      |              |                  |                                |                          |
|      |                                      |              |                  |                                |                          |
|      |                                      |              |                  |                                |                          |
|      |                                      |              |                  |                                |                          |
|      |                                      |              |                  |                                |                          |
|      |                                      |              |                  |                                |                          |
|      |                                      |              |                  |                                |                          |
|      |                                      |              |                  |                                |                          |
|      |                                      |              |                  |                                |                          |
|      |                                      |              |                  |                                |                          |
|      |                                      |              |                  |                                |                          |

# Yearly Maintenance Log

| Date | Smoke Detector Batteries | Carbon Monoxide Detector | Clean Gutters | Other: | Other: | Performed By (Initials) |
|------|--------------------------|--------------------------|---------------|--------|--------|-------------------------|
|      |                          |                          |               |        |        |                         |
|      |                          |                          |               |        |        |                         |
|      |                          |                          |               |        |        |                         |
|      |                          |                          |               |        |        |                         |
|      |                          |                          |               |        |        |                         |
|      |                          |                          |               |        |        |                         |
|      |                          |                          |               |        |        |                         |
|      |                          |                          |               |        |        |                         |
|      |                          |                          |               |        |        |                         |
|      |                          |                          |               |        |        |                         |
|      |                          |                          |               |        |        |                         |
|      |                          |                          |               |        |        |                         |
|      |                          |                          |               |        |        |                         |
|      |                          |                          |               |        |        |                         |
|      |                          |                          |               |        |        |                         |
|      |                          |                          |               |        |        |                         |
|      |                          |                          |               |        |        |                         |
|      |                          |                          |               |        |        |                         |

# Yearly Maintenance Log

| Date | Smoke Detector Batteries | Carbon Monoxide Detector | Clean Gutters | Other: | Other: | Performed By (Initials) |
|------|--------------------------|--------------------------|---------------|--------|--------|-------------------------|
|      |                          |                          |               |        |        |                         |
|      |                          |                          |               |        |        |                         |
|      |                          |                          |               |        |        |                         |
|      |                          |                          |               |        |        |                         |
|      |                          |                          |               |        |        |                         |
|      |                          |                          |               |        |        |                         |
|      |                          |                          |               |        |        |                         |
|      |                          |                          |               |        |        |                         |
|      |                          |                          |               |        |        |                         |
|      |                          |                          |               |        |        |                         |
|      |                          |                          |               |        |        |                         |
|      |                          |                          |               |        |        |                         |
|      |                          |                          |               |        |        |                         |
|      |                          |                          |               |        |        |                         |
|      |                          |                          |               |        |        |                         |
|      |                          |                          |               |        |        |                         |
|      |                          |                          |               |        |        |                         |

# Yearly Maintenance Log

| Date | Smoke Detector Batteries | Carbon Monoxide Detector | Clean Gutters | Other: | Other: | Performed By (Initials) |
|------|--------------------------|--------------------------|---------------|--------|--------|-------------------------|
|      |                          |                          |               |        |        |                         |
|      |                          |                          |               |        |        |                         |
|      |                          |                          |               |        |        |                         |
|      |                          |                          |               |        |        |                         |
|      |                          |                          |               |        |        |                         |
|      |                          |                          |               |        |        |                         |
|      |                          |                          |               |        |        |                         |
|      |                          |                          |               |        |        |                         |
|      |                          |                          |               |        |        |                         |
|      |                          |                          |               |        |        |                         |
|      |                          |                          |               |        |        |                         |
|      |                          |                          |               |        |        |                         |
|      |                          |                          |               |        |        |                         |
|      |                          |                          |               |        |        |                         |
|      |                          |                          |               |        |        |                         |
|      |                          |                          |               |        |        |                         |
|      |                          |                          |               |        |        |                         |
|      |                          |                          |               |        |        |                         |

# Notes

# Notes

# Notes